Seven Natural Wonders of
AUSTRALIA and
OCEANIA

Michael Woods and Mary B. Woods

TWENTY-FIRST CENTURY BOOKS

Minneapolis

*To John and Catherine Woods
and Joseph and Mary Boyle*

Twenty-First Century Books
A division of Lerner Publishing Group, Inc.
241 First Avenue North
Minneapolis, MN 55401 U.S.A.

Website address: www.lernerbooks.com

Library of Congress Cataloging-in-Publication Data

Woods, Michael, 1946–
    Seven natural wonders of Australia and Oceania / by Michael Woods and Mary B. Woods.
        p.   cm. — (Seven wonders)
    Includes bibliographical references and index.
    ISBN 978–0–8225–9074–3 (lib. bdg. : alk. paper)
    1. Natural history—Australia. 2. Landforms—Australia. I. Woods, Mary B. (Mary Boyle), 1946– II. Title
QH196.8.W66 2009
508.94—dc22   2008014003

Manufactured in the United States of America
1 2 3 4 5 6 – DP – 14 13 12 11 10 09

Contents

1
2
3
4
5
6
7

INTRODUCTION

PEOPLE LOVE TO MAKE LISTS OF THE BIGGEST AND THE BEST. ALMOST 2,500 YEARS AGO, A GREEK WRITER NAMED HERODOTUS MADE A LIST OF THE MOST AWESOME THINGS EVER BUILT BY PEOPLE. THE LIST INCLUDED BUILDINGS, STATUES, AND OTHER OBJECTS THAT WERE LARGE, WONDROUS, AND IMPRESSIVE. LATER, OTHER WRITERS ADDED NEW ITEMS TO THE LIST. WRITERS EVENTUALLY AGREED ON A FINAL LIST. IT WAS CALLED THE SEVEN WONDERS OF THE ANCIENT WORLD.

The list became so famous that people began imitating it. They made other lists of wonders. They listed seven wonders of the modern world and seven wonders of the Middle Ages. People even made lists of undersea wonders.

People also made lists of natural wonders. Natural wonders are extraordinary things created by nature, without help from people. Earth is full of natural wonders, so it has been hard for people to choose the absolute best. Over the years, different people have made different lists of the Seven Wonders of the Natural World.

A red kangaroo hops through the Australian Outback.

4

This book explores seven natural wonders from Australia and Oceania. Australia is a country and a continent in the South Pacific Ocean. Oceania is the general name given to the many islands of the Pacific. Like Earth as a whole, Australia and Oceania have far more than seven natural wonders. But even if people can never agree on which ones are the greatest, these seven choices are sure to amaze you.

A WONDERFUL ADVENTURE

Australia is the world's smallest, flattest, and driest continent. Millions of years ago, it broke off from a huge landmass called Gondwana. The break isolated the continent, and Australia developed its own unique and extraordinary nature.

Oceania stretches from Micronesia in the west to Polynesia in the east. Spread across the vast expanses of the Pacific, Oceania's islands have also developed extraordinary plants, animals, and land formations.

This book will take you on a tour of some of the region's natural wonders. The tour will include a few stops in Australia for a glimpse of its amazing life and natural landmarks. In Oceania you will land on lush tropical islands, walk to the edge of an active volcano *(below)*, and climb a mountain that keeps losing its peak. These fascinating places are waiting. Read on to begin your adventure.

Lava from Kilauea sprays high into the air.

1 THE *Australian Outback*

An Australian Outback landscape

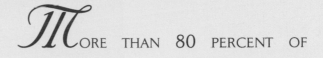ORE THAN 80 PERCENT OF AUSTRALIA'S 20 MILLION PEOPLE LIVE ALONG THE COUNTRY'S COASTS. MOST LIVE IN OR NEAR A FEW COASTAL CITIES. THE VAST INTERIOR OF AUSTRALIA INCLUDES 2.5 MILLION SQUARE MILES (6.5 MILLION SQUARE KILOMETERS) OF LAND. BUT LESS THAN 10 PERCENT OF THE POPULATION LIVES THERE. MUCH OF THE INTERIOR IS A HUGE, FLAT, DRY EXPANSE OF LAND. AUSTRALIANS SOMETIMES CALL IT THE BUSH, THE BACK OF BEYOND, OR THE NEVER NEVER. BUT THE WHOLE REGION IS MOST WELL KNOWN AS THE OUTBACK. AND AS SUNBAKED AND EMPTY AS MUCH OF IT SEEMS, THE OUTBACK IS FULL OF AMAZING THINGS.

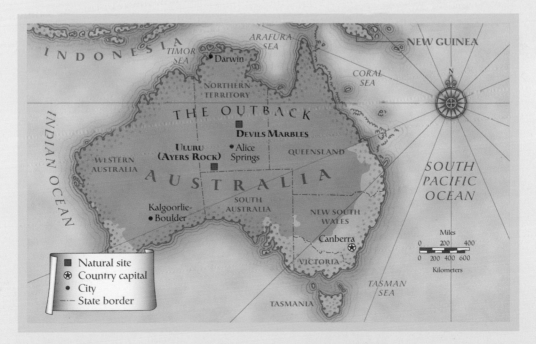

WIDE OPEN LAND

Australia is divided into states and territories—the Australian Capital Territory, Victoria, New South Wales, Queensland, the Northern Territory, South Australia, and Western Australia. The northwest corner of New South Wales, more than half of Queensland and South Australia, and almost all the Northern Territory and Western Australia are part of the Outback.

Some Outback residents live in towns such as Alice Springs and Kalgoorlie-Boulder. But almost 70,000 Australians live in very remote areas away from any big towns. Many work in the mining industry. The soil beneath the Outback contains rich mineral deposits, including gemstones. In other Outback regions, enough grass grows to feed livestock. In these places, families work isolated sheep and cattle farms called stations.

MEASURING THE *Back of Beyond*

The Outback has no real borders and no exact size or location. Most of the Outback is usually thought of as the dry, interior desert. But it can include the fringes of woodlands and rain forests. Australians use the word *Outback* to mean any sparsely populated region, away from large cities. The Australian government lists Outback areas as outer regional, remote, or very remote. The definitions are based on how far people live from their nearest neighbor and how far away they are from services such as doctors, dentists, and schools.

An Australian farmer uses a helicopter to move his cattle on the Outback. Farms in the Outback have to be large to support the families who live on them.

FLYING Doctors

When people in the Outback get sick, they call for a flying doctor. Since 1928, airplanes have been flying doctors and nurses to help people in the Outback. These medical professionals work for the Royal Flying Doctor Service of Australia. The service provides emergency care for people who are injured or very sick. Air ambulances may fly those patients to hospitals in cities such as Alice Springs and Darwin. Flying doctors and nurses also make regular visits to the Outback to give people checkups.

Neighbors in these parts of the Outback are few and far between. Some people own small planes instead of cars because they have to travel such long distances to towns. Imagine having to fly to the grocery store! Doctors and other health-care workers have to fly into the Outback. And children "attend" school by using special radios or the Internet. Life in the Outback often consists of a lot of hard work, with few chances to socialize.

In spite of the hardships, the Outback figures large in the history and culture of Australia. For Aborigines, Australia's native people, the Outback is their homeland. Aborigines have lived in the Outback for forty thousand years. They are one the world's oldest continuous societies. The Outback is sacred to the Aborigines. The sites, plants, and animals are a part of their religion and mythology.

European explorers first reached Australia in the 1600s. British ships arrived in 1788 and established the first settlement in New South Wales. The settlers took another twenty-five years to begin exploring Australia's interior. For these British and Irish settlers, the Outback was a frontier—Australia's Wild West. The landscape and the blazing heat must have been as strange to them as being on another planet. But the hardworking pioneers and tough cattle ranchers pressed on across the land.

"Many of the oldest objects ever found on earth—the most ancient rocks and fossils, the earliest animal tracks and riverbeds, the first faint signs of life itself—have come from Australia."

—*U.S. travel writer Bill Bryson in his 2000 book on Australia,* In a Sunburned Country

The Europeans discovered what the Aborigines had always known—that the Outback was filled with wonders. And those wonders still draw photographers, wildlife experts, geologists (scientists who study Earth's soil and rocks), and tourists from all over the world.

ULURU (AYERS ROCK)

Alice Springs is known as the capital of the Outback. The city has about 25,000 residents. It is located in the Northern Territory, in the center of the most remote part of Australia. Like much of the Outback, Alice Springs has a harsh climate. The area gets barely 12 inches (30 centimeters) of rain each year. Temperatures average 100°F (37.8°C) in summer. Winter temperatures average 40.5°F (4.7°C).

Alice Springs is the closest city to some of the Outback's most famous natural wonders. One of those wonders is Uluru, also known as Ayers Rock. This mountainlike chunk of stone stands about 270 miles (440 km) southwest of Alice Springs. It is part of Uluru-Kata Tjuta National Park.

Uluru-Kata Tjuta National Park is known worldwide for its natural beauty, unusual geology, and cultural importance. Uluru itself is Australia's most famous landmark. It is famous for its size and unusual reddish glow.

The park is on land traditionally owned by the Anangu Aboriginal people. Uluru is a sacred place to the Anangu. They believe

THE SCHOOL of the Air

Alice Springs has an unusual school. It includes all the students in an area of 502,000 square miles (1.3 million square km). That's larger than the states of Texas, Arizona, and New Mexico combined.

Fewer than 200 students live in that enormous area. They certainly don't ride the bus to school—that would take days! These students learn at home. They attend Alice Springs School of the Air (ASSOA).

In the 1940s, Adelaide Miethke, a teacher, came up with the idea of broadcasting lessons on the radio. Classes were held over the airwaves— giving the school its name.

Modern ASSOA classes use new technology. Students and teachers communicate on high-tech radios (below), satellite networks, and the Internet.

ancestor beings made the land, animals, and people many ages ago during the Tjukurpa, or Creation Time. Creation Time is also sometimes called Dreamtime or the Dreaming. Uluru is one of the extraordinary places created during the Tjukurpa.

The rock is about 1,132 feet (345 meters) tall—the size of a twelve-story building. It is 2.2 miles (3.6 km) long and 1.2 miles (2 km) wide. A person walking around the base of Uluru would cover a distance of 5.8 miles (9.4 km).

Scientists believe Uluru rose above the Outback hundreds of millions of years ago. Uluru is made of sandstone—grains of sand and stone packed together until they form rock. It also contains feldspar, a mineral often found in sandstone. Iron in Uluru's feldspar gives the rock its reddish color. At sunset, light reflects off the dust and minerals and gives Uluru a bright red glow.

In 1987 Uluru-Kata Tjuta National Park was named a World Heritage site by the United Nations Educational, Scientific, and Cultural Organization (UNESCO). UNESCO World Heritage sites are natural sites, monuments, and buildings of outstanding value to world history and culture.

The Australian Outback

The park draws more than 400,000 visitors every year. The park's Cultural Centre offers information on Anangu culture and history and on Uluru's geology. Many visitors, with Anangu guides, make the four-hour trek around Uluru's base. And of course, most tourists bring their cameras—Uluru is one of the most photographed spots in Australia.

THE DEVILS MARBLES

The Northern Territory's Outback is home to another amazing rock formation—the Devils Marbles. These huge red, rounded granite stones are about 244 miles (393 km) north of Alice Springs. They are part of the Devils Marbles Conservation Reserve.

The biggest of the marbles are 23 feet (7 m) across. Amazingly, these round rocks stay in place. Some lie in piles. Others are balanced on narrow ridges. But they do not topple over and roll away.

Scientists think that the marbles started to form millions of years ago. At that time, a single block of granite covered Earth's surface in this area. The granite cracked and split into smaller blocks.

Rain and windblown sand gradually eroded, or wore away, the edges of the blocks. Over time, the blocks became rounded. Erosion is still at work on blocks of rock in the reserve. Some newly cracked blocks have sharp edges. Others that cracked long ago are more rounded.

Like Uluru, the Devils Marbles are part of Aboriginal beliefs. According to legend, an ancestor being called the Rainbow Serpent created mountains and other land formations during Creation Time. After creation, the

A boulder rests on top of another at the Devils Marbles Conservation Reserve. The reserve—a protected area run by the Northern Territory government—includes 4,453 acres (1,802 hectares) of remote land.

Rainbow Serpent went to the central desert and laid many eggs. Over time, those eggs turned to stone. Aboriginal people named them Karlukarlu. When Europeans first saw the rocks, they called them the Devils Marbles.

A red kangaroo and her joey (baby) watch for predators.

OUTBACK WILDLIFE

The Outback's wonders are not limited to rock formations. It also has some one-of-a-kind plant and animal life. About 80 percent of Australia's plants and animals are found nowhere else in the world. Many of the Outback's plants and animals are specially adapted to the extremely dry, hot climate. Some animals can go for days without food and water. Others have found ways to keep their bodies from overheating.

Kangaroos are the Outback's most famous animals. Australia has more than fifty kinds of kangaroos. They range in size from the 1-pound (0.5 kilogram) musky rat-kangaroo to the 130-pound (60 kg) red kangaroo. The red kangaroo is a symbol of Australia. Images of this Outback animal appear on Australia's coat of arms (a national emblem) and on some of its coins.

Another animal often seen in the Outback is a wild dog called the dingo. Dingoes are closely related to wolves. They have been breeding with domestic (tame) dogs for many years. But they have kept some of their wild ways. For example, they hunt for their food in packs of about fifteen. And they like to howl at night, as their wolfish relatives do.

Koalas are also native to the Outback. Koalas are small mammals—about 2 feet (0.6 m) tall and weighing from 15 to 30 pounds (7 to 14 kg). Koalas like to sleep a lot. They sleep up to eighteen hours a day. With their peaceful faces and slow pace, koalas are often compared to cuddly teddy bears. People sometimes even call them koala bears, although koalas are not related to bears.

Emus might be less cuddly, but they are just as interesting. At almost 6 feet (2 m), emus are the second-tallest bird in the world. (The tallest is the African ostrich.) Emus have long necks, fluffy feathers, and three toes on each foot. They are strong animals and can run up to 30 miles (48 km) an hour. Like the kangaroo, the emu appears on Australia's coat of arms and on coins.

Emus are not Australia's only famous birds. The eastern edges of the Outback are home to kookaburras. Kookaburras are known for the very unusual sounds they make. Their calls often sound like human laughter. Kookaburras start their calls very early in the morning. They are so loud that they wake up nearby humans. This habit has earned the birds the nickname of the bushman's clock.

Australia also has sixty species of parrots. Many live in the rain forests of northern Queensland. But others have adapted to live in colder areas to the south and drier areas with fewer trees. Their varied habitats means that Australian parrots have a wide range of sizes and colors. They range from large white cockatoos to small blue budgerigars—and almost every color in between.

THE DINGO *Fence*

Sheep are one of the dingo's favorite foods, and dingo packs will raid sheep stations in search of a meal. This habit has made the wild dogs into a serious pest for sheep farmers. In fact, as far back as the 1880s, Australians put up wire fencing to keep dingoes away from areas with many sheep stations. The Dingo Fence *(below)* grew to be more than 3,000 miles (5,000 km) long, stretching across southeastern Australia. It is the longest fence in the world.

Top left: *A dingo listens for danger.* Top right: *A koala sits in a eucalyptus tree.* Bottom left: *A kookaburra sits on a branch.* Bottom right: *An emu can weigh from 65 to 120 pounds (30 to 54 kg).*

OUTBACK PLANTS

The Outback's flora (plant life) is plentiful and unique. It has evolved to survive in heat, strong sun, and without rainfall. The flora has also adapted to grow back after the region's frequent bushfires. Bushfires are wildfires often caused by extremely dry conditions or by lightning.

For the few hours a day when it is awake, the koala likes to munch on the leaves of eucalyptus trees. The trees also provide food and shelter to birds, animals, and insects. Eucalyptus are also called gum trees. Australia has more than 700 kinds. The tallest kinds can grow to be 328 feet (100 m) tall. Eucalyptus leaves have a very strong smell. Oil from the leaves is used in medicines (such as cold medicine) and ointments sold around the world.

In drier parts of the Outback, acacia trees are common. Acacia trees are also called wattles. Australia has almost nine hundred kinds of acacia. They vary from low shrubs to tall, spreading trees. Many kinds of acacia have bright yellow or golden flowers. Flowering acacia branches are pictured on Australia's coat of arms.

Outback flora also includes many types of short shrubs and grasses. Hummock and tussock are two types of grasslands. Hummock grasses grow in small, rounded mounds. They provide a habitat for birds, reptiles, and animals such as the wallaby (a small type of kangaroo). Tussock grasses grow in clumps and are taller and less common than hummock grasses. Sheep and cattle eat

SOME *Sweetheart!*

Saltwater crocodiles *(below)*, or salties, are the most dangerous animals in the Outback. These reptiles are found along the northern coast of Australia. Salties grow to a length of more than 20 feet (6 m). Some weigh as much as a small car. When salties come near beaches, lifeguards post signs to warn swimmers. People must stay out of the water or risk being eaten. In the 1970s, one salty started attacking fishing boats near the city of Darwin. Its body was put out on display in a Darwin museum. People jokingly named this fierce croc Sweetheart.

Golden wattle is a common flowering tree in Australia.

OUTBACK *Camels*

More than 500,000 camels roam the Outback. But they are not native animals. European settlers first imported camels to Australia from places such as India in the mid-1800s. These hardy desert animals can go for days without water and can carry heavy loads.

Camel caravans carried materials needed to build Alice Springs. They carried materials to build railroad lines and telegraph lines across the continent. Camel trains also brought supplies into remote mining towns and ranches.

When cars and trucks became common in the 1900s, camels no longer were needed. Camel owners let the animals loose. Camels now run wild. They can be seen along with wild horses, which are called brumbies.

tussock grasses. Wildflowers and other plants grow in among the grasses. Even in the driest parts of the Outback, visitors can see blazes of color in the flora.

OUTBACK PRIDE

With easy air travel, better roads, and better communication systems, the Outback is less of an isolated frontier than it was in the past. But it remains a rugged and unique land. It attracts millions of tourists from around the world each year. Many are willing to drive great distances through the heat and dust to tour Uluru or catch a glimpse of a kangaroo family.

For Australians the Outback remains at the heart of Aboriginal beliefs and the whole country's history. And through songs, legends, novels, movies, photographs, and documentaries, Australia has shared the wonders of the Outback with the rest of the world.

2 Aoraki/ Mount Cook

Aoraki/Mount Cook rises in the South Pacific country of New Zealand.

*A*ORAKI / MOUNT COOK IS A
TOWERING MOUNTAIN IN THE SOUTH PACIFIC COUNTRY OF NEW
ZEALAND. AT MIDNIGHT ON DECEMBER 14, 1991, IT WAS 12,349
FEET (3,764 M) HIGH. A FEW MINUTES LATER, AORAKI/MOUNT
COOK WAS 33 FEET (10 M) SHORTER.

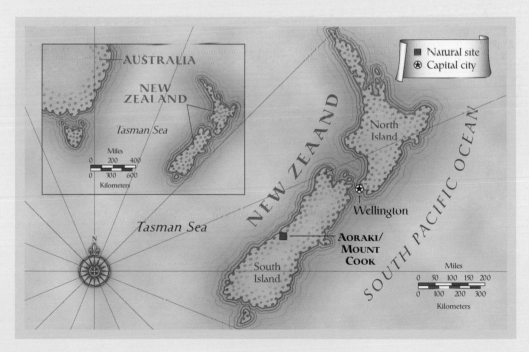

A gigantic avalanche, or rock fall, took off the top of Aoraki/Mount Cook. Rocks, soil, and ice at Aoraki/Mount Cook's peak broke loose. They tumbled down the mountainside in a rumbling whoosh. The mountain lost as much height as a three-story building.

Aoraki/Mount Cook has been losing its head this way for millions of years. Powerful forces inside Earth push this amazing mountain up. It grows higher and higher. Then an avalanche topples its peak.

If all the rock, soil, and ice had stayed put over the centuries, Aoraki/Mount Cook would be the highest mountain on Earth. Scientists say that the mountain would be at least 65,000 feet (20,000 m) high. That's more than twice the size of Mount Everest, the world's highest mountain.

Aoraki/Mount Cook is the highest mountain in New Zealand. New Zealand is about 1,250 miles (2,000 km) southeast of Australia. The country consists of two large islands and several small islands. The two main islands are called the North Island and the South Island. Aoraki/Mount Cook is located on the South Island. It is one of many high peaks in a mountain range called the Southern Alps.

Aoraki/Mount Cook is one of the Southern Alps in New Zealand. The Southern Alps run along the western side of the South Island.

RUBBING *Noses*

Some people say hello by shaking hands. Others greet one another with a hug or a kiss. The Maori rub noses. Maori call this greeting the *hongi.* That means "sharing of breath."

Maoris perform a traditional action song. The Maori have worked hard to revive their traditional culture.

A MOUNTAIN WITH TWO NAMES

Captain John Lort Stokes (1812–1885) gave the mountain one of its names. In 1851 this British naval officer was sailing along the coast of New Zealand. Stokes saw a towering mountain. He named it Mount Cook after British explorer Captain James Cook (1728–1779). In the 1770s, Cook was among the first Europeans to explore and map parts of New Zealand and Australia.

European settlers in New Zealand used Stokes's name for the mountain. But Europeans were not the first people in New Zealand, and Mount Cook already had a name. The Maori were New Zealand's first people. They had lived on the islands for more than one thousand years. The Maori name for Mount Cook was Aoraki. In the Maori language, *Aoraki* means "cloud piercer."

The Maori called New Zealand *Aotearoa.* That word means "the land of the long white cloud." Maori people traditionally lived in villages. They hunted wild animals and gathered wild plants as food. They also grew crops, including potatoes and kumaras (a sweet potato).

Maori culture has many forms of art. The people carve beautiful objects from wood, bone, and stone. They weave designs into cloth. Maori group performances, called *kapa haka,* involve dancing, singing, and music.

Aoraki/Mount Cook

21

> *"If I should bow my head,*
> *let it be to a high mountain."*
>
> —*Maori proverb*

During the 1800s, British settlers filled New Zealand. They built towns and set up farms. New Zealand became a part of the British Empire, and a British-style government was established. The British signed a treaty (a political agreement) with Maori leaders. But much of the Maori culture was pushed aside as New Zealand became more European. British settlers soon broke their treaty and took away most Maori land.

In the early 1900s, some Maori people began a movement to reclaim their traditions and culture. They took up many traditional art forms again. And they pushed the government to return their lands. It took several decades, but by the late 1900s, the country was doing more to honor New Zealand's Maori heritage. That effort included renaming Mount Cook. In 1998 the New Zealand government combined the mountain's Maori and British names into Aoraki/Mount Cook.

MAKING A MOUNTAIN

The ancient Maori had no written language. They remembered the past with stories passed from one generation to another. One of those stories tells how Aoraki/Mount Cook was formed.

The story is about a young boy named Aoraki. While paddling a canoe, Aoraki and his three brothers accidentally crashed into rocks. The canoe got stuck, with one end tilted up into the sky.

Aoraki and his brothers climbed to the high side. As they sat in the wreckage, a cold wind began to blow. That wind froze the boys. They turned

EVER *Wonder?*

Why does Aoraki/Mount Cook have a gray color? The mountain is made from a dark-colored rock called greywacke (pronounced gray-wacky). Greywacke contains sandstone. Scientists think greywacke built up around the edges of Gondwana. When Gondwana broke up and moved north, greywacke was deposited on the ocean floor. It hardened and was later pushed upward to form New Zealand's mountains.

In 1990 Aoraki/Mount Cook, Westland, Fiordland, and Mount Aspiring National Parks were combined as a UNESCO World Heritage site. The site is called Te Wahipounamu-South West New Zealand.

into stone and became the Southern Alps, the mountain range that includes Aoraki/Mount Cook.

Scientists see an echo of geologic truth in that ancient story. They say that Aoraki/Mount Cook and the rest of the Southern Alps were formed when two gigantic plates of rock collided about 25 million years ago.

Earth's surface is made up of huge sheets of rock called tectonic plates. These plates drift slowly on a layer of soft rock deep below the surface. Where two plates meet, the edges grind against each other with enormous force.

Aoraki/Mount Cook formed at the place where the Australian Plate and the Pacific Plate collided. That point is along New Zealand's western edge. The Pacific Plate slid under the Australian Plate, pushing up giant slabs of rock to form the Southern Alps. Aoraki/Mount Cook has been pushed up about 65,617 feet (20,000 m) over the last fifteen million years.

The uplifting continues. It raises Aoraki/Mount Cook about one-quarter inch (0.7 cm) each year. However, Aoraki/Mount's Cook's rock cracks very easily. Erosion from water and wind makes the rock crumble. Rock slides and avalanches wear away the top of Aoraki/Mount Cook almost as fast as it is pushed up.

PARK OF WONDERS

In 1953 the New Zealand government established a national park that includes Aoraki/Mount Cook. Aoraki/Mount Cook National Park has about 175,000 acres (70,696 hectares) of land.

Aoraki/Mount Cook National Park contains nineteen peaks that are almost 10,000 feet (3,000 m) high. More than 140 of its mountains tower more than 6,500 feet (2,000 m). Like Aoraki/Mount Cook, many of those mountains are coated with gleaming white snow year-round.

Some of the snow that falls on the mountains never melts. Instead, it collects on snowfields and on thick glaciers (ice sheets). The glaciers are like rivers of ice that slowly flow down the mountainsides. Aoraki/Mount Cook National Park has more than seventy glaciers.

Long ago, the glaciers helped give these mountains their rugged peaks and jagged sides. As a glacier flows, it picks up rocks, almost like a snowball rolling in the dirt. The rocks freeze into the bottom of the glacier. So as the glacier flows, it acts like sandpaper. The glacier carves grooves into the mountainside. As glaciers move down the mountains into warmer weather, some of their ice melts. These rivers of ice turn into rivers of water or into glacial lakes.

Aoraki/Mount Cook National Park's largest glacier is the Tasman Glacier. It is 18 miles (29 km) long and in some places is 2 miles (3 km) wide. The glacier flows down the eastern side of Aoraki/Mount Cook. Melting ice from the glacier formed Lake Tasman.

A WONDER FOR ALL

With its towering mountain, glaciers, and fields of snow that never melt, Aoraki/Mount Cook National Park might sound like a cold and harsh place. But most of the park is an alpine terrain. *Alpine* refers to areas high in the mountains, but not so high that nothing grows there. The park has a wide variety of plants and animals. Some are found only in New Zealand. In summer the park's fields are filled with Mount Cook buttercups, an alpine flower. Mountain daisies and a spiky grass called wild Spaniard are also common.

The kea, or mountain parrot, makes its home in the park. These beautiful birds have olive

THREE
Kiwis

The kiwi is a flightless bird *(below)* about the size of a chicken. It has grayish-brown feathers and a long beak. This unusual-looking animal is New Zealand's national bird. A "kiwi" also is a nickname for a person from New Zealand. And the word has a third meaning—the name of a fruit. Kiwifruits are a little larger than a chicken's egg. They have a sweet green center. Kiwifruit originated in New Zealand.

green feathers and blue green tails. They are large, about the size of a chicken. Keas eat mainly berries, plant leaves, and insects.

Aoraki/Mount Cook National Park is a popular place for visitors. About 500,000 New Zealanders and foreign tourists visit the park each year. Visitors walk, hike, and ride horses through the alpine areas. Those with the skills and equipment climb the park's mountains. Visitors can also fish or boat on the glacial lakes. And many skiers take to the slopes, even skiing out onto the glaciers. At the center of it all, of course, is Aoraki/Mount Cook—one of New Zealand's greatest natural wonders.

Left: *Mount Cook buttercups are found only in New Zealand.* Below: *A climber scales an icy cliff on the Tasman Glacier.*

3 Mount Kilauea

Mount Kilauea
erupts in Hawaii.

$\mathcal{W}$HEN MANY PEOPLE THINK OF THE HAWAIIAN ISLANDS, THEY THINK OF SWIMMING IN WARM WATERS, SUNBATHING ON WHITE-SAND BEACHES, AND SIPPING ICY DRINKS IN THE SHADE OF PALM TREES. THE ISLANDS ARE A TROPICAL PARADISE IN THE NORTH CENTRAL PACIFIC.

But Hawaii is more than just sun and sand. The island chain is also home to a fiery and dangerous natural wonder—Kilauea. Kilauea is one of the world's most active volcanoes.

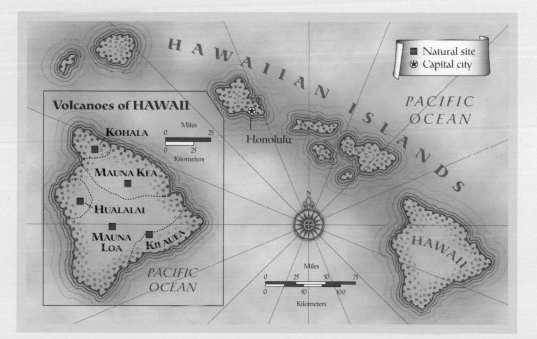

PELE'S VOLCANO

Kilauea sits on the southeastern edge of the island of Hawaii, also known as the Big Island. (Hawaii is the name of the U.S. state that includes all the Hawaiian Islands and is also the name of the largest island in the group.) Kilauea is not the only volcano on the Big Island. It is not even the largest. Two nearby volcanoes, Mauna Loa and Mauna Kea, are much bigger. But Kilauea is an important volcano. In ancient legends, it is home to Pele, the Hawaiian goddess of volcanoes.

People have lived in Hawaii for thousands of years. The first people to settle in the islands were from islands in the South Pacific. Traditional Hawaiian culture includes many legends of gods and goddesses. In Hawaiian myth, Pele lives inside Kilauea. She decides when the volcano will erupt.

Eruptions can be frightening and very dangerous. During an eruption, red-hot melted rock called lava flows out of volcanoes. Volcanoes also may send rocks, ashes, and gas shooting high into the air. Eruptions may kill people living nearby and destroy homes, schools, and other buildings.

For these reasons, Pele has a reputation as a goddess with a fierce temper. Many stories explain how and why Pele's temper makes Kilauea erupt. But the science behind the volcano is just as amazing as the legends.

EUROPEAN *Discovery*

Europeans first learned about Hawaii after Captain James Cook landed on the island in 1778. This English explorer had also sailed around Australia and New Zealand. Cook called the Hawaiian Islands the Sandwich Islands after a wealthy English nobleman, the Earl of Sandwich.

The first European at Kilauea was the Reverend William Ellis. Ellis was a missionary, or religious teacher. His mission was to bring the Christian religion to Hawaii's local peoples. Ellis climbed Kilauea in 1823. After Ellis's visit, Europeans began tracking the volcano's activity.

"We stopped and trembled."
—British missionary William Ellis, who stood on the edge of Mount Kilauea in 1823 and wrote the first English-language description of the volcano

ISLANDS ON A PLATE

In the Hawaiian language, *kilauea* means "spewing" or "much spreading." Lava from Kilauea spreads down the mountainsides and into the sea. Scientists think that this volcano has been spewing lava for 300,000 to 600,000 years. Kilauea is one of a series of volcanoes that formed the Hawaiian Islands.

The islands formed on the Pacific Plate. The Pacific Plate is the tectonic plate that lies beneath the Pacific Ocean. Tectonic plates drift slowly on Earth's crust. The Pacific Plate moves about 4 inches (10 cm) a year.

Each island formed as the Pacific Plate moved over a hot spot in Earth's crust. At hots pots, heat escapes from deep inside Earth. The heat melts rock. The melted rock pours out through an undersea volcano. As it hits the water, the melted rock cools and hardens. The hardened rock piles up around the undersea volcano.

Over thousands of years, the volcano gets higher and higher. Eventually, the volcano's top rises above the ocean surface as an island. The Hawaiian Islands are the tops of undersea volcanoes. They formed almost in a line, one by one, as the Pacific Plate moved to the northwest over the hot spot.

Lava from Kilauea meets the sea and creates a cloud of steam.

Because of that motion, the oldest Hawaiian islands are in the northwest. The youngest, including Hawaii, are in the southeast. The hot spot produced several gigantic volcanoes, including Mauna Loa, Mauna Kea, and Kilauea.

Mauna Kea is the highest. It rises 13,796 feet (4,205 m) above sea level. Mauna Kea has not erupted for hundreds of years. Mauna Loa is 13,680 feet (4,170 m) high. It erupted several times in the 1900s.

KILAUEA'S LAVA

Kilauea emerged from the sea more than 50,000 years ago. Located on the side of Mauna Loa, Kilauea is about 4,190 feet (1,277 m) high. Kilauea has been erupting since it emerged from the ocean. The volcano's most recent activity began in 1983. Kilauea has been erupting almost continually since then.

Some volcanoes explode during their eruptions. Sudden blasts of lava, searing hot gas, and ash kill people and destroy the surrounding land. Kilauea usually is a gentle giant. The lava flows slowly and quietly down from the volcano. But Kilauea's lava sometimes spouts up in great fountains. The fountains have reached a height of more than 1,000 feet (300 m).

The lava flows can damage property and hurt people. But usually people have plenty of time to move out of the way. Scientists in the Hawaii Volcano Observatory near the top of Kilauea keep watch on the volcano. They issue a warning to the public when dangerous eruptions are about to happen.

Kilauea releases enormous amounts of lava. Since 1983 Kilauea has released almost 2 billion cubic yards (1.5 billion cu. m) of lava. That's enough lava to make a two-lane highway 1.25 million miles (2 million km) long. Such a road would circle Earth fifty times.

DEADLY *Eruptions*

Mount Kilauea is not always a gentle giant with mild eruptions. This volcano has turned violent in the past and could again in the future. During a 1790 eruption, an explosion sent hot gas and rocks shooting out of the volcano. Dozens of people were killed. During a 1924 eruption, hundreds of explosions sent rocks the size of school buses hurling through the air. Some boulders flew for two-thirds of a mile (1 km). The explosion killed one person.

*Scientists research
and document
Kilauea. Red-hot
lava flows nearby
through a lava tube.*

In 1990 a lava flow from Kilauea destroyed the towns of Kalapana and Kaimu. The lava covered several beaches and a large section of State Route 130. The highway came to a dead end at the lava flow.

MAKING NEW LAND

Some volcanoes are cone shaped. They are called stratovolcanoes. But Kilauea has a gentle sloped shape, like a hill. Volcanoes with this shape are known as shield volcanoes. Many of the largest volcanoes on Earth are shield volcanoes.

Shield volcanoes get their sloping shape from lava flows. The lava from shield volcanoes is almost all basalt, a type of rock. When cool, basalt is very dense and hard. But heated up as lava, it is a free-moving liquid. Basalt flows from the summit of a volcano in all directions. As it cools, it hardens. Flow after flow builds up the lava as new land. The entire island of Hawaii is made up of five shield volcanoes—Kilauea, Mauna Loa, Mauna Kea, Hualalai, and Kohala—and their flows.

PELE'S TEARS *and Hair*

Several forms of lava are named for the volcano goddess, Pele. Pele's tears are small drops of lava that cool in the air into teardrop-shaped rocks. Pele's hair consists of thin, brittle strands of volcanic glass. These strands form as hot lava flows into the colder Pacific Ocean.

A WORLD *Heritage Site*

Hawaii Volcanoes National Park was named a UNESCO World Heritage site in 1987 for its unique geology and landscape.

In addition to these five volcanoes, a new volcano is growing off the coast of the Big Island. About 19 miles (30 km) south of Kilauea, the Loihi Seamount is growing on the ocean floor. Loihi is an active volcano. Eruptions add to the volcano and often cause a series of small undersea earthquakes called earthquake swarms. The lava has built up to a height of 3,179 feet (969 m) below the surface. At the present rate, scientists think Loihi will emerge as an island within 200,000 years.

VISITING PELE'S HOME

Kilauea is part of the Hawaii Volcanoes National Park. It is the most popular tourist attraction in this part of Hawaii. Tourists can tour Crater Rim Drive, an 11-mile (18 km) road that encircles the top of the volcano. The road runs through different landscapes, including desert and lush tropical rain forest. Visitors can also hike or take walks with park ranger guides.

Visitors are a threat to some natural wonders. Tourists may damage plants or disturb animals in a natural habitat. But Kilauea can be a threat to tourists, who often don't know what to expect from an active volcano. People with breathing problems can be hurt by Kilauea's gases. Some hikers have been burned by getting too close to hot lava. Others cut themselves on sharp bits of newly hardened lava. Park rangers recommend that visitors first stop at the Kilauea Visitor Center to learn about and enjoy this amazing wonder.

A lava flow blocks Chain of Craters Road in Hawaii Volcanoes National Park.

"Here and there were gleaming holes a hundred feet [30 m] in diameter, broken in the dark crust, and in them melted lava—the color a dazzling white tinged with yellow—was boiling and surging furiously. . . . "
— U.S. writer Mark Twain, describing Kilauea in 1866

4 THE *Bungle Bungles*

The Bungle Bungles are sandstone cones in Western Australia.

*I*N 1982 A TELEVISION STATION SENT OUT A CAMERA CREW TO LOOK FOR UNDISCOVERED NATURAL WONDERS IN AUSTRALIA. THE STATION WANTED THE CREW TO SEARCH THE STATE OF WESTERN AUSTRALIA. IN THOSE DAYS, THE NORTHERN PARTS OF THE STATE WERE UNEXPLORED TERRITORY TO MOST WHITE AUSTRALIANS. THE CREW TRAVELED BY PLANE BECAUSE FEW ROADS LED INTO THE STATE'S OUTBACK.

As the camera crew flew over the wilderness, they passed the small town of Kununurra. They flew south a while longer. Then suddenly, they looked down and could not believe their eyes. Spread out over the desert were hundreds of natural stone cones. Stranger still, the beehive-shaped formations were striped orange and black. The crew had found their new natural wonder—the Bungle Bungles.

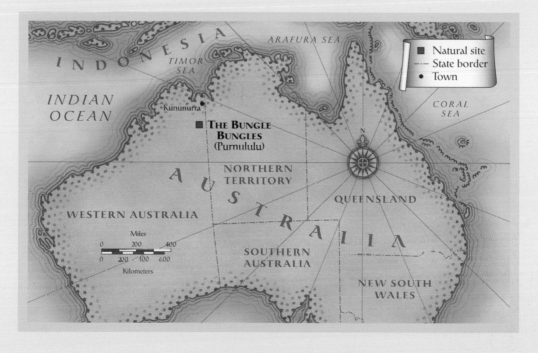

PURNULULU

The Bungle Bungles might have been new to most Australians, but Aboriginal people had always known about them. The Kija are one group of Aboriginals who live in that region. They call the enormous land formation Purnululu. *Purnululu* is the Kija word for sandstone—the soft rock that forms the Bungles. The name *Bungle Bungles* might come from someone

FROM *the Air*

Some visitors say the best way to see the Bungle Bungles is from the air. That viewpoint shows the true size, shape, and colors of the natural scenery. Visitors can take tours in helicopters or in small airplanes.

Many photographs of the Bungle Bungles are taken from small planes and helicopters. These aerial views show the Bungles' amazing beehive shapes and colors.

> "The Bungle Bungles are by far the most outstanding example of [such] sandstone anywhere in the world."
>
> —UNESCO, in naming Purnululu National Park a World Heritage site, 2002

DOWN *Under*

Australia lies in the Southern Hemisphere, on the other side of the globe from Europe, most of Asia, and North America. British settlers in Australia began calling the country the land down under. Because Australia is "down under" on the globe, some things are opposite from those in northern countries. For example, the farther north you get in Australia, the hotter the climate becomes. Northern Australia is closer to the equator than southern Australia. The seasons are also reversed. Autumn is from March to May, and winter is from June to August. Spring begins in September, and summer runs from December to February. Christmas is one of the first holidays of the Australian summer.

incorrectly hearing an Aboriginal word. Or it might have come from a common plant found in the region, bundle bundle grass.

In Aboriginal beliefs, stories tell how the world began. Ancient Aborigines did not have a written language to record those legends. But storytelling was an important part of their culture. Aborigine adults told stories about events in the past. Young people listened, remembered, and passed the stories along to their children.

The legend about how the Bungle Bungles formed involved the giant Rainbow Serpent. In Aboriginal mythology, this huge snake emerged from the earth during Dreamtime—when ancient ancestor spirits were busy creating the world. The Rainbow Serpent slithered across the land. As its body wiggled, the snake created valleys and mountains. Some of those mountains became the Bungle Bungles.

For thousands of years, the Kija have lived in this area. Their ancient ancestors made paintings on the sides of cliffs and other rocks. Some paintings show scenes from their legends. Some pictures show emus, kangaroos, and other Outback animals. The pictures show how important

the Bungle Bungles were to those first residents of the region. The region and the legends about it remain important to modern Aborigines.

MAKING THE BUNGLES

The Bungle Bungles are a range of small sandstone mountains. The mountains stand about 200 feet (61 m) to 300 feet (91 m) above a plain. The range is located about 160 miles (257 km) south of Kununurra. This land of grassland and forest is part of the Kimberley, a section of Western Australia.

It took almost twenty million years of erosion from water and rain to form the Bungle Bungles. The mountains formed from the bed of an ancient sea that dried up. Forces deep inside Earth pushed the seabed upward into a plateau. A plateau is a flat table of raised land. Cracks split the plateau into huge chunks.

Over the ages, rivers and streams flowed through the cracks. The water slowly wore away the soft sandstone in the sides of the cracks. Wind and rain caused more erosion. Eventually erosion carved the plateau into towers of rock. Erosion gradually smoothed the sides of the towers into beehive shapes.

The black stripes on the Bungle Bungles are caused by the growth of lichen. These plantlike organisms are a type of fungus that grows on top of the sandstone. Dark-colored algae then grow on top of the fungus. The orange bands result from thin layers of iron and manganese oxide, two metals found in the sandstone.

Crusts of lichen and metals do more than give the Bungle Bungles tiger stripes. The crust also protects the soft stone, almost like a coat of paint. Without the lichen, rain and wind would continue wearing away the Bungles. Eventually, the mountains would break apart into bits of sand and rock and disappear.

PURNULULU NATIONAL PARK

In 1987 the Australian government made the Bungle Bungles and the surrounding area into a national park. As part of a national park, the environment and animals of the region are protected. To honor the Aborigines, the government named the park Purnululu National Park.

The park covers an area of 930 square miles (2,400 sq. km). It is almost the size of the state of Rhode Island. In addition to the striped cones of the Bungle Bungles, the park includes plains, grasslands, and forested areas. High cliffs plunge into steep-sided valleys such as Cathedral Gorge, Piccaninny Gorge, Echidna Chasm, and Frog Hole. In the wet season (November to March), waterfalls drop down into clear pools and fan palms sway in the hot breezes.

Many kinds of animals live in the park—reptiles, mammals, amphibians, and fish. Purnululu also has more than 130 species of birds. Some of them, such as the gray falcon, are very rare. The park is home to several kinds of wallaby. Another relative of wallabies and kangaroos, the wallaroo, also lives in the area.

RAINBOW Bee-Eaters

Rainbow bee-eaters are beautiful birds that live in Purnululu National Park. These brightly colored birds have brilliant blue, green, and orange feathers. Their slender black bills (beaks) are perfect for scooping up bees and wasps. A single bee-eater can scarf down more than two hundred bees in one day. Before swallowing, they rub each bee against a tree branch or rock to remove the stinger.

WORRIES ABOUT THE WONDER

The Bungle Bungles may look very strong. But their soft sandstone is delicate and crumbles easily. To prevent damage, the park does not allow people to climb in certain areas. No one is allowed to dig into the mountains or to construct buildings in the park. Beyond the national park, the government established a buffer zone to the north and west. Rules protecting the natural environment apply to the 309-square-mile (800 sq. km) buffer zone.

Purnululu National Park's location also helps preserve these wonders. It is far away from big cities and difficult to reach. In 1986 a nearby highway was built. But to get into the park, visitors must drive over difficult terrain in four-wheel-drive vehicles. Campers must carry in their own food and water and must camp only in certain areas. Those who do travel to the park enjoy the isolated beauty and learn about the area from the local Aboriginal people.

In 2003 UNESCO added Purnululu National Park to its list of World Heritage sites. It named the park's outstanding natural beauty and importance in understanding Australia's geology. In 2004 Western Australia celebrated the 175th anniversary of its founding as a colonial settlement. To mark the occasion, the government of Western Australia named the Bungle Bungles a heritage icon—a symbol of the state's culture and history.

WOLFE CREEK *Crater*

About 125 miles (200 km) southwest of Purnululu National Park is another amazing wonder—Wolfe Creek Crater. The crater lies in the desert at the edge of the Kimberley region. The crater was formed 300,000 years ago when a meterorite—a huge rock from outer space—crashed into Earth. Scientists think the crater was originally about 400 feet (120 m) deep—deep enough to hold a thirty-story building. Over the ages, the crater filled with sand until it was about 200 feet (60 m) deep from the rim to the floor. At 2,880 feet (880 m) across, it is the second-largest crater in the world (after Vredefort Crater in South Africa).

This natural amphitheater is at the head of Cathedral Gorge in Purnululu National Park.

THE TASMANIAN
Wilderness

Cradle Mountain is reflected in a lake in the Tasmanian Wilderness.

*T*ASMANIA IS THE ONLY AUSTRALIAN STATE THAT IS NOT PART OF THE COUNTRY'S MAINLAND. TASMANIA IS AN ISLAND 150 MILES (240 KM) SOUTH OF THE SOUTHEASTERN TIP OF THE CONTINENT. HOBART IS THE CAPITAL AND LARGEST CITY OF TASMANIA. OF TASMANIA'S 494,000 RESIDENTS, MORE THAN 40 PERCENT LIVE IN HOBART. THERE ARE NO OTHER BIG CITIES. MUCH OF THE REST OF THE STATE REMAINS A NATURAL ENVIRONMENT— PROTECTED BY NINETEEN NATIONAL PARKS AND 420 WILDERNESS RESERVES. THE TASMANIAN WILDERNESS WORLD HERITAGE AREA (WHA) IS ONE OF AUSTRALIA'S GREATEST NATURAL WONDERS.

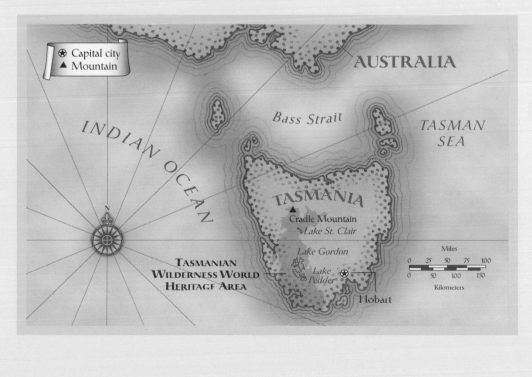

A NATURAL BEAUTY

Wilderness is land that is natural, full of wild plants and native animals. Few people live in the wilderness, and there are no cities, farms, or shopping centers. The world still has many large areas of wilderness. Almost half Earth's land is wilderness. Canada has vast forestlands. Africa has the enormous Sahara. In the Arctic region and Antarctica, there is snow and ice as far as the eye can see.

Tasmania's WHA is different from many other wilderness areas. It is part of a temperate climate. In fact, Tasmania contains one of the world's largest remaining areas of temperate wilderness. Temperate areas are not hot and dry like deserts. Nor do they see extreme amounts of rain and snow. These areas have a change of seasons and generally mild weather.

Almost one-fifth of Tasmania consists of this type of wilderness. The WHA is located in the southwestern part of the state. It covers 5,342 square miles (13,836 sq. km). The area includes three national parks—Franklin-Lower Gordon Wild Rivers National Park, Southwest National Park, and Cradle Mountain-Lake St. Clair National Park—and other preserves.

A WILD WONDERLAND

The WHA is a place of stunning natural beauty. One part of the

Rain forests, such as this one surrounding Cradle Mountain, are places of lush plant and animal life.

Huon pines grow very slowly. Most grow less than 0.08 inches (2 millimeters) in diameter each year.

wilderness has become a symbol of that wild beauty. It is near Cradle Mountain and Lake St. Clair.

Cradle Mountain's jagged peaks rise to a height of about 5,068 feet (1,545 m). Ice-cold streams flow down the mountain through grassy meadows and valleys. Surrounding the mountain is a wild landscape of ancient rain forests, ponds, and lakes.

On sunny days, a postcard-perfect image of Cradle Mountain reflects on the surface of Lake St. Clair. With a depth of more than 600 feet (183 m), it is Australia's deepest lake.

The most famous hiking trail in Australia runs between those two wonders. The Overland Track extends for 40 miles (65 km). Hikers along the trail pass through the heart of the WHA.

Rain forests in the WHA include amazing plants and animals. Rare Huon pine trees, for instance, are among the world's oldest trees. Some reach an age of almost three thousand years.

"It is magnificent. Everyone should know about it and come and enjoy it."

—*Austrian scientist Gustav Weindorfer, describing Cradle Mountain in the Tasmanian wilderness in 1910*

This suspension bridge over the Franklin River is part of the Overland Track.

A forest of swamp gum trees, also known as eucalyptus regnans

ENDANGERED *Devils*

Since the 1990s, wildlife researchers have tracked a disease that threatens the Tasmanian devil *(below)*. Called the devil facial tumor disease (DFTD), it causes cancerous growths on the animal's face, especially around the mouth. DFTD prevents devils from eating, and they starve to death. DFTD is one of the few cancers than can spread from animal to animal. In some parts of the wilderness, DFTD has killed about 90 percent of adult Tasmanian devils. Researchers are working to control and prevent DFTD. But in the meantime, Tasmanian devils have become endangered— animals in danger of dying out as a species.

The Styx Valley sometimes is called the Valley of the Giants. It is home to the world's tallest hardwood trees. They are swamp gum trees. These giants reach a height of almost 290 feet (88 m). Some are more than four hundred years old. The trees produce clusters of white flowers about 0.5 inches (1 cm) wide.

Tasmania has some amazing animals too. One of the most famous is the Tasmanian devil. Tasmanian devils are only about the size of small dogs. The animal got its name because of some of its characteristics. They don't smell very good, they screech loudly, and they bite when disturbed. The devils, though, are an important part of Tasmania's natural environment. They are scavengers—animals that feed on carrion (dead animals)—and will eat anything from dead wallabies to dead birds. And they eat every bit of their food—bones, teeth, fur. In doing so, they help keep the habitat clean.

VAN DIEMAN'S LAND

Europeans first became aware of Tasmania in 1642. A Dutch explorer named Abel Tasman sighted the islands while on an expedition. Tasman gave the islands their first name—Van Diemen's Land. That name honored Anthony van Diemen, a Dutch ruler who sent Tasman on his voyage.

Other explorers visited Van Diemen's Land over the years. But in general, Europeans paid little attention to this remote place. That changed in 1803, when Great Britain established a settlement at the present-day city of Hobart.

In those days, Great Britain had very harsh laws. Courts severely punished people for small crimes. More than two hundred crimes carried the death penalty. A person who stole a loaf of bread or a chicken could be sentenced to years in prison.

Prisons in Great Britain got crowded, with no room for more prisoners. The government began sending prisoners to Australia. The first penal, or prison, colony was established in present-day Sydney. The second penal colony was built on Van Diemen's Land.

MARVELOUS *Marsupials*

Tasmania and other Australian states are home to a group of animals called marsupials. Baby marsupials are born when they are very tiny. They cannot live in the outside world. After birth, they crawl into a special pocketlike pouch on their mother's belly. That pouch, the marsupium, gives newborn marsupials a safe place to grow.

More than 260 kinds of marsupials exist. They include kangaroos, wallabies *(right)*, wallaroos, koalas, Tasmanian devils, wombats, and bandicoots. Most marsupials are found only in Australia, New Zealand, and parts of Indonesia.

"*Too far South for spices and too close to the rim of the earth to be inhabited by anything but freaks and monsters.*"

—*Dutch explorer Abel Tasman, describing Tasmania, the island that was named for him in 1642*

A wallaby feeds on shrubs on the Overland Trail. Cradle Mountain is in the distance.

Of course, the island was not empty when the prisoners, guards, and laborers arrived. Nine groups of Aborigines already lived in Van Diemen's Land. Almost all the Aborigines were killed by European diseases and in violent clashes with the British settlers. All around, it was a harsh life in a wild land.

Few settlers then thought of wilderness areas as beautiful places. Dangerous wild animals roamed through some of these areas. The animals sometimes attacked and killed settlers. And with no roads or maps, it was easy to get lost in the deep wilderness.

People wanted civilization, ease, and progress. Prisoners and settlers began to cut down trees in wild areas. They built roads and railroads to make travel easier. Ranchers brought in herds of cattle to graze on plants in wild areas. Farmers cleared wild land to grow crops.

TAKING CARE OF THE WILDERNESS

Great Britain stopped sending prisoners to Van Diemen's Land in 1853. In 1856 the island was renamed Tasmania. In 1901 Great Britain granted political independence to Australia. It became its own country, and Tasmania became a state.

As the 1900s wore on, Tasmanians began to worry that too much wilderness was disappearing. They realized that their country's wilderness was unique and important. These areas were the last remains of the natural world that existed on Earth for millions of years.

By spending time in wilderness areas, people could connect with the past. The peaceful natural environment gave them a break from the stress of everyday life. Gradually, people took action to protect the remaining wilderness areas.

For example, in the late 1970s, some people wanted to build a dam in the WHA. That dam would have blocked a river. Instead of flowing freely, the river water would collect behind the dam and form a lake. That lake would have flooded huge areas of wild land. The government of Australia stopped construction of the dam.

ENJOYING THE WONDER

In 1989 the Australian government joined together the national parks that became the WHA. UNESCO named the wilderness a World Heritage site in 1989. The area sees more than 25,000 visitors every year. Visitors hike, horseback ride, and fish.

Tasmania's Parks and Wildlife Service works hard to preserve the natural beauty of the WHA. Rules govern certain activities in the region. Permits are needed to explore the WHA's caves. Bikes and cars are not allowed in certain areas. Some rules about where to go and not to go are meant to protect visitors, too—it is still very easy to get lost in the deepest parts of this natural wonder.

The sun rises over Lake St. Clair in the WHA.

6 Bora Bora

Bora Bora is an island in the South Pacific Ocean.

WILD REGIONS OF LAND COME IN

ALL SHAPES AND COLORS—FROM THE RED EARTH OF THE OUTBACK

TO THE LUSH GREEN OF A TASMANIAN RAIN FOREST. BUT THERE IS

ANOTHER KIND OF WILDERNESS IN OCEANIA, AND IT DOESN'T EVEN

INVOLVE LAND. THE PACIFIC OCEAN IS THE WORLD'S LARGEST AND

DEEPEST OCEAN. IT COVERS ALMOST ONE-THIRD OF EARTH. MUCH

OF THE SOUTH PACIFIC IS A WILDERNESS OF WATER—THOUSANDS OF

MILES OF OPEN SEA BROKEN ONLY BY TINY ISLANDS.

One of those islands is Bora Bora. With its beautiful weather and scenery, it has been called the most perfect island in the world. And its plants and wildlife make it one of the natural wonders of Oceania.

Tropical Islands

Many of Oceania's islands in the South Pacific are uninhabited. Nothing much can grow or live there. Other islands are the tips of volcanoes. Those islands are usually larger and are home to a wide variety of life.

Most Pacific islands lie between the tropics of Cancer and Capricorn. Many lie close to the equator. The tropics are imaginary lines used on maps and globes. The equator is the imaginary line that divides the globe in half horizontally, cutting through South America, Africa, and Indonesia.

Below the Tropic of Cancer, Pacific islands are divided into three groups—Melanesia, Micronesia, and Polynesia. *Melanesia* means "dark islands." *Micronesia* means "small islands." And *Polynesia* means "many islands." Each island group has its own features and unique cultures. Many different groups of people live on the islands, and all together they are known as Pacific islanders.

Bora Bora is part of Polynesia. It lies in the region known as French Polynesia. For most people in the world, Bora Bora is a faraway paradise. It is about 2,600 miles (4,183 km) south of Hawaii. An airplane flight from New York City to Bora Bora would take more than thirteen hours.

The closest large island to Bora Bora is Tahiti. Also a French Polynesian island, Tahiti is about 160 miles (257 km) from Bora Bora. Big airplanes land in Tahiti. Passengers then board smaller planes for the flight to Bora Bora.

Forming an Island

Bora Bora is one of French Polynesia's Society Islands. The Society Islands were formed about seven million years ago as the Pacific Plate passed over a hot spot in Earth's crust. The lava from undersea volcanoes cooled, hardened, and built up until the volcano tops rose above the surface of the Pacific. Tahiti and Bora Bora are among the largest of the fourteen volcanic Society Islands.

Bora Bora is tiny. The total area of land is only 17 square miles (44 sq. km). From

The Society *Islands*

The Society Islands are divided into two groups—the Leeward Islands and the Windward Islands. Bora Bora is a Leeward Island. In French the Windward Islands are called *Îles du Vent*—literally "islands of wind." The Leeward Islands are the *Îles sous le Vent*—islands under the wind. *Leeward* also means "sheltered from the wind" in English.

the air, the island looks emerald green. The green is broken by two dark mountains—the tips of Bora Bora's ancient undersea volcano. Mount Pahia is smooth and rounded. It rises to a height of 2,159 feet (658 m). The other, Mount Otemanu, has sharp, rugged sides. Otemanu is 2,385 feet (727 m) high and the highest point on Bora Bora.

The island is encircled by a pale blue green lagoon. A lagoon is a shallow body of water separated from the ocean. Bora Bora's lagoon is separated from the surrounding Pacific waters by a barrier reef. The reef is formed from living corals. These marine animals have an outer skeleton of calcium carbonate—the same substance seashells are made of. As corals die, they leave behind their skeletons. Newer corals grow on top of the dead coral, and the reef builds up underwater.

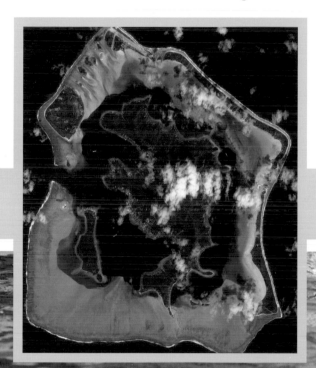

Left: *Bora Bora's lagoon and barrier reef are easy to see in this satellite image.* Below: *The barrier reef is a colorful habitat for many plants and animals.*

A forest of coconut palms covers Bora Bora.

A NATURAL PARADISE

Bora Bora's green color comes from thousands of coconut palms and other trees. The island's coconut palms grow to heights of almost 100 feet (31 m). Some of their fanlike leaves grow to lengths of 19 feet (6 m). Each palm may produce more than seventy coconuts per year.

Polynesia is famous for its tropical flowers. On Bora Bora, hibiscus plants bloom in among the lush greenery. Their large flowers bloom in several colors, from white to deep pink.

Not many land animals live on Bora Bora. The Polynesian islands are far away from other landmasses, so few land animals have ever reached the island. But Bora Bora has many tropical birds. And the lagoon and surrounding Pacific Ocean are full of marine life. Corals, crabs, and brilliantly colored tropical fish fill the blue waters.

The waters are also home to a very unusual sea creature—the giant manta ray. A manta ray's body is almost flat. It looks almost like a giant bat swimming underwater. Rays may grow to be more than 15 feet (5 m) from side to side. Some weigh as much as a car.

Some old legends tell of fierce giant mantas attacking and overturning fishing boats. Those legends earned manta rays the nickname of devilfish. But mantas are actually gentle. Scuba divers and snorkelers sometimes swim next to manta rays without being harmed.

Left: *A stingray swims in the waters off Bora Bora.* Above: *Hibiscus flowers color the island.* Below: *Green sea turtles swim with fish in the lagoon.*

BORA BORA'S HISTORY

Pacific islanders have lived on Bora Bora for at least 1,500 years. Legends say that the first people arrived on Bora Bora by boat. They may have come from Tonga or other Polynesian islands. According to local beliefs, the supreme god Taaroa first created the island of Raiatea. Raiaeta gave birth to Bora Bora. The ancient islanders called Bora Bora *Mai Te Pora*. That means "created by the gods." They also called it simply Pora Pora, or "first born."

A Dutch explorer, Jacob Roggeveen, was the first European to land on Bora Bora. Roggeveen arrived on the island in 1722. He was on an expedition searching for Australia.

At that time, Europeans thought that a very large continent must exist in the Southern Hemisphere. Without it, they thought Earth would be out of balance, since there was so much land in the Northern Hemisphere.

Europeans called this unknown continent Terra Australis, or "land of the south." Roggeveen never found Australia. But he did find several Polynesian islands, including Bora Bora. When Roggeveen and his crew heard the island's local peoples pronounce Pora Pora, they mistook the *P* sound for a *B*. They began calling the island Bora Bora.

Other European visitors followed Roggeveen to Polynesia. British navigator Samuel Wallis came in 1767. French navigator Louis-Antoine de Bougainville arrived in 1768. And British explorer James Cook first saw Bora Bora during a 1769 expedition. All described a paradise of blue lagoons and lush plant life. News of Polynesia's natural beauty spread through Europe.

In the 1800s, France took over the Polynesian islands and made them into a French colony. The French allowed some local Polynesian rulers to keep their titles. But they were forced to give up any real power.

Ships carrying whale hunters and traders began coming to Polynesia. So did Chinese workers hired to labor on plantations (large farms). Some plantations

> *"They have likewise around their houses a kind of kitchen garden in which they plant potatoes, yams, and other roots. . . . Their soil . . . is the most fertile in the universe."*
>
> —French explorer Louis-Antoine de Bougainville, describing the Polynesian people, 1768

grew cotton. Others grew the fragrant fruit of a tropical orchid. That fruit is picked and processed to make vanilla, a flavoring used in foods and perfumes.

Other laborers worked on coconut plantations. Coconut trees are very useful. They provide the coconut used in cookies, cakes, and other food. Dried coconut meat is called copra. It contains coconut oil, which is used to make skin creams, soaps, and foods.

BORA BORA DURING WAR

In 1939 World War II began in Europe. This conflict involved many countries. France, Great Britain, and other countries fought against Germany. In the Pacific, Germany's ally Japan had begun invading other Asian countries. The fighting grew nearer and nearer to the west coast of the United States. In December 1941, Japan attacked U.S. naval ships at Pearl Harbor, Hawaii. The United States declared war on Japan.

The U.S. military started to build military bases with airplane runways on some Pacific islands. Warplanes and soldiers used these bases in the war against Japan. In 1942 the United States built a military base on Bora Bora.

A gun from World War II (1939–1945) rusts on the hills of Boru Bora.

About 5,000 U.S. soldiers were based on Bora Bora. The island was an important supply base, but no battle was ever fought on the island. The war ended in 1945, and the next year, the U.S. military closed the base. Many of the U.S. soldiers were sorry to leave Bora Bora behind. They had fallen in love with the island's natural beauty. Their stories helped make Bora Bora and the rest of French Polynesia famous in the United States.

STILL A PARADISE

Bora Bora remains famous for its natural beauty. The island attracts thousands of visitors each year. About 9,000 people live on the island, and most of them make a living in some part of the tourism business. Some work in hotels and some in restaurants. Others work as tour guides.

Tourists can drive or ride bikes around the island on a road built by World War II soldiers. Visitors can also swim, scuba dive, and go snorkeling. Special guided trips allow visitors to swim alongside manta rays and sharks. Tourists can stay in island hotels or in huts built on stilts over the water.

Tourism is the island's biggest business, but it can also be damaging to Bora Bora. Laws limit how many new hotels can be built and how close they can be built to the water. Rules also protect the island's bird, plant, and marine life. Island residents know that they must take care to protect and preserve Bora Bora's natural wonders.

Tourist bungalows built on stilts over the lagoon are a famous feature of Bora Bora.

LOVE THAT *Island!*

Stories say that some U.S. soldiers fell in love with Bora Bora while based there during World War II. They might have liked the island a little too much. When the war ended, they did not want to go home. Stories say the military police had to force some soldiers to leave their adopted tropical paradise.

"The most beautiful island in the world. . . ."

—U.S. writer James A. Michener, describing Bora Bora, 1947

7 New Caledonia

The island country of New Caledonia
is in the South Pacific Ocean.

$\mathcal{T}$HE OLDEST FLOWERING PLANT SPECIES STILL ALIVE GROWS IN ONLY ONE PLACE ON EARTH. THAT PLANT IS AMBORELLA, AND IT GROWS WILD ON THE ISLAND NATION OF NEW CALEDONIA IN THE SOUTH PACIFIC. AMBORELLA IS A SMALL SHRUB WITH TINY GREENISH YELLOW FLOWERS AND RED FRUIT. IT HAS GROWN ON NEW CALEDONIA FOR AT LEAST 130 MILLION YEARS. NEW CALEDONIA IS AN AMAZING TREASURE CHEST OF SUCH ANCIENT, RARE PLANTS.

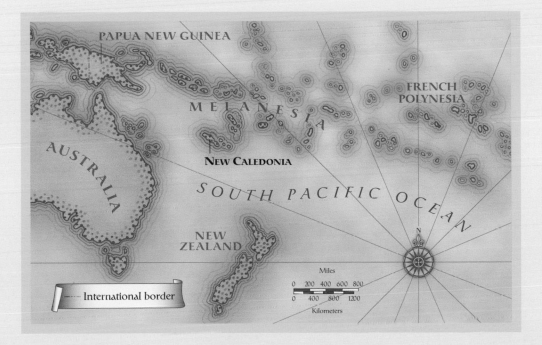

> *"Amborella . . . has one attribute that makes it perhaps the most interesting plant of all. It has survived for at least 130 million years."*
> —writer Cheryll Greenwood Kinsley, describing this living fossil in 2000

TINY TREASURE TROVE

New Caledonia is one of the world's richest areas of biodiversity. *Biodiversity* means "a variety of plant and animal life." An area known for biodiversity has an unusually wide range of life. That wide range may include plants and animals that live only in that one place.

New Caledonia is a small country—only the size of the state of New Jersey. It lies in Melanesia in the Pacific, 750 miles (1,200 km) east of Australia. About 222,000 people live in New Caledonia.

New Caledonia's main island is called Grande Terre ("big land" in French). The rest of the country is made up of smaller islands—the Loyalty Islands, Belep Island, the Surprise Islands, and the Isle of Pines. Farther away are the Chesterfield Islands, tiny Matthew Island, and Hunter Island.

A large variety of plants are found on the islands of New Caledonia. This picture was taken on Lifou Island, which is one of the Loyalty Islands.

The Isle of Pines is the southernmost island of New Caledonia.

Grande Terre is 217 miles (350 km) long and between 31 and 44 miles (50 and 70 km) wide. It has the only high land in New Caledonia. A mountain range runs through the center of Grande Terre. Five of the mountains are more than 4,950 feet (1,500 m) high.

This island is an original piece of Gondwana, the supercontinent that once existed in the Southern Hemisphere. Gondwana was home to many different prehistoric plants and animals. It had dinosaurs, for instance, and giant evergreen trees.

Gondwana began to break up about 175 million years ago. Its pieces drifted apart. They became India, Australia, Africa, South America, and Antarctica. Smaller pieces of land broke off from those masses.

One of those small pieces was Grande Terre. It separated from Australia about 85 million years ago. Grande Terre became a separate landmass. The island drifted into its present place about 55 million years ago.

LAND OF LIVING FOSSILS

Scientists call many of New Caledonia's plants living fossils. The island's plants are the same plants that grew during the age of the dinosaurs. Dinos such as the *Tyrannosaurus rex* lived more than 65 million years ago. Like dinosaurs, most plants from prehistoric times became extinct.

We know about these prehistoric animals and plants only from fossils. Fossils are the remains of animals and plants preserved in rock and other materials. In prehistoric times, floods covered dead dinos with mud. The mud and dinosaur bones hardened into the fossils that we see in museums. In the same way, plant leaves left imprints in mud. The mud hardened, producing plant fossils.

But New Caledonia's plants and animals did not end up as dead imprints. As the island drifted away from the rest of Gondwana, it served as a sort of museum. It saved Gondwana's original prehistoric plants and animals. They were isolated from other plants and animals. They became living fossils—records of past life on Earth that scientists can study.

When organisms become isolated, they can only reproduce among themselves. They cannot mix with other plants and animals. That isolation helped give New Caledonia species that are very different from those found elsewhere in the world.

New Caledonia, for instance, has about 3,270 plant species. Seventy-four percent of those plants—about 2,430 species—are found only in New Caledonia.

Some belong to a group of prehistoric trees called araucarias. These living fossils can grow to be 200 feet (60 m) tall. Araucaria branches grow in dense rings around a narrow tree trunk. Only nineteen species of araucaria still exist in the world. Thirteen of those are found only in New Caledonia.

About one hundred species of birds live on New Caledonia. More than twenty exist only on New Caledonia. One is a bird named the kagu. About the size of a chicken, the kagu is mainly a ground bird.

MONKEY Puzzle Tree

One kind of araucaria tree is famous for its name—the monkey puzzle tree. The tree was first brought back to England in the late 1700s and planted in gardens *(below)*. According to legend, someone was touring an English garden and noticed a tree with many swirling branches very close together. The person remarked that even a monkey would be puzzled at how to climb such a tree. From then on, that type of araucaria was called the monkey puzzle tree.

> *"I feel like I'm walking in a forest the dinosaurs knew."*
> —scientist Eric Dinerstein, describing New Caledonia in 2000

It has feathers and wings, but it does not fly for long distances. The kagu is the national bird of New Caledonia.

More than sixty of New Caledonia's seventy reptiles are found nowhere else in the world. Most of them are geckos and other lizards. The New Caledonian giant gecko is the most famous. It is one of the world's largest geckos. This creature can grow up to 11 inches (28 cm) long and weigh up to 1.5 pounds (0.7 kg). Many other species of amphibians, insects, and other animals are found only in New Caledonia.

Left: *The kagu is one of the twelve rarest birds in the world.* **Below:** *A New Caledonia giant gecko spends most of its life in the forest canopy (top branches).*

KANAKY

Pacific islanders have lived on New Caledonia for thousands of years. About three thousand years ago, the Kanaks arrived from New Guinea (an island to the northwest). The Kanaks settled in different parts of Grande Terre and on New Caledonia's other islands. Each group developed a distinct culture, and about twenty different languages were spoken on the islands.

James Cook was the first European to see Kanaky. Cook reached Grande Terre while on an expedition in 1774. Grande Terre reminded Cook of some rugged areas of Scotland. Scotland's Latin name is Caledonia, so Cook named the island New Caledonia. Local peoples call the land Kanaky.

New Caledonia became a colony of France in 1853. The French colonial government ruled the islands. In 1956 New Caledonia became an overseas territory of France. This change meant that New Caledonians began to govern themselves to a certain degree. But France still controls areas such as immigration, the military, and relations with foreign countries. Many residents hope New Caledonia will become an independent nation within a few years.

LOYAL *Islands*

In the 1700s, British trading ships stopped at some of New Caledonia's small islands. The islands had no name at that time. The sailors picked a name. They thought that the local people on these islands were kind and friendly. Sailors named the islands the Loyalty Islands in honor of the kind residents.

Residents of New Caledonia swim in one of its natural swimming pools.

Worries about the Wonder

Many of New Caledonia's residents depend on the island's mineral wealth. One of those minerals is an ore, or rock, used to make nickel. A silvery white metal, nickel is added to other metals to make them strong and long lasting. New Caledonia has the largest-known deposits of nickel ore in the world. Its mines produce almost half of the world's nickel. New Caledonia also has rich iron and manganese mines.

Nickel mining provides many New Caledonians with work. But it also causes one of the biggest worries about New Caledonia's natural wonders. Nickel in New Caledonia is taken from open-pit mines. At these mines, workers use giant earthmoving machines to dig into the surface of the land. The machines damage or kill trees.

Evergreen rain forests once covered almost 70 percent of New Caledonia. In the 2000s, rain forests occupy only about 20 percent of the land. These forests are disappearing due to open-pit mining and other human activities. The only remaining untouched prehistoric forests are found in the central mountains.

Other issues threaten New Caledonia's biodiversity. People, for instance, have brought animals that never lived on New Caledonia in the past. Those animals include ship rats, goats, pigs, dogs, and cats. They threaten the animals present naturally in New Caledonia.

Some of the animals run wild and hunt birds. For instance, wild dogs have killed all but a few hundred kagu. Goats and pigs also damage native plants. Environmental groups are working to stop the damage. They have named New Caledonia a biodiversity hot spot. Environmentalists and scientists know that once the rare living fossils are gone from New Caledonia, they are gone forever. Environmental groups and residents are working to preserve New Caledonia's unique natural heritage.

Nickel mines dot the landscape of New Caledonia.

TIMELINE

CA. 175 million B.C.	The supercontinent of Gondwana begins to break up and drift north, forming Australia and other southern continents.
CA. 55 million B.C.	The piece of Gondwana that forms New Caledonia's main island drifts into place in Melanesia.
CA. 7 million B.C.	The Society Islands form in the South Pacific Ocean.
CA. 50,000 B.C.	Aboriginal peoples reach Australia from Southeast Asia. Mount Kilauea emerges from the sea.
CA. 1,000 B.C.	Kanaks settle on New Caledonia.
CA. A.D. 500	Maori settlers reach New Zealand from other Pacific islands.
1600s	European explorers first reach Australia.
1642	Dutch explorer Abel Tasman first sees the west coast of Tasmania. He calls the island Van Dieman's Land.
1722	Dutch explorer Jacob Roggeveen is the first European to land on Bora Bora.
1769	British explorer Captain James Cook sees Bora Bora.
1770s	Cook maps parts of New Zealand and Australia.
1774	Cook becomes the first European to see New Caledonia. He names the island after the Latin word for Scotland.
1778	Cook lands on the islands of Hawaii and names them the Sandwich Islands.
1788	British settlers arrive in modern-day New South Wales.
1790	A violent eruption of Kilauea kills dozens of people.
1800s	France makes Polynesian islands into a French colony.
1803	Great Britain establishes a prison settlement at the present-day city of Hobart, Tasmania.
1823	British missionary William Ellis climbs Kilauea. Ellis's visit marks the beginning of modern tracking of Kilauea's volcanic activity.
1850s	Settlers introduce camels to Australia to carry building materials and supplies to the Outback.
1851	British naval officer John Lort Stokes first sees Aoraki in New Zealand and names it Mount Cook.
1856	Van Dieman's Land is renamed Tasmania.
1880s	Australians begin building the world's longest fence to keep dingoes away from sheep stations.

1901   Great Britain grants independence to Australia.

1924   An eruption of Kilauea kills one person and sends huge boulders flying.

1928   Australia's Royal Flying Doctor Service begins providing medical services to remote areas of the Outback.

1942   The United States builds a military base on Bora Bora during World War II.

1946   Adelaide Miethke develops the idea behind Australia's School of the Air.

1953   New Zealand's government establishes Aoraki/Mount Cook National Park.

1982   A television news crew spots the Bungle Bungles in the northern part of Western Australia.

1983   Kilauea's most recent eruption activity begins.

1987   UNESCO lists Uluru-Kata Tjuta National Park and Hawaii Volcanoes National Park as World Heritage sites. The Australian government establishes Purnululu National Park.

1989   The Australian government joins together several national parks and nature reserves as the Tasmanian Wilderness. UNESCO names the wilderness a World Heritage area.

1990   Te Wahipounamu-South West New Zealand (Aoraki/Mount Cook, Mount Aspiring, Westland, and Fiordland National Parks) is named a UNESCO World Heritage site. Lava from Kilauea destroys the Hawaiian towns of Kalapana and Kaimu.

1991   An avalanche shaves 33 feet (10 m) off the top of Aoraki/Mount Cook.

1995   The Australian government changes Ayers Rock-Mount Olga National Park to Uluru-Kata Tjuta National Park.

1998   New Zealand's government combines the English and Maori names for the mountain into Aoraki/Mount Cook.

2003   UNESCO adds Purnululu National Park to its list of World Heritage sites.

2004   Western Australia celebrates its 175th anniversary and names the Bungle Bungles a heritage icon.

2008   UNESCO adds the lagoons of New Caledonia to its list of World Heritage sites.

CHOOSE AN EIGHTH WONDER

Now that you've read about the seven natural wonders of Australia and Oceania, do a little research to choose an eighth wonder. Or make a list with your friends, and vote to see which wonder is the favorite.

To do your research, look at some of the websites and books listed in the Further Reading and Websites section of this book. Look for places in Australia and Oceania that
- *are especially large*
- *are exceptionally beautiful*
- *were unknown to foreigners for many centuries*
- *are unlike any other place on Earth*

You might even try gathering photos and writing your own chapter on the eighth wonder!

GLOSSARY AND PRONUNCIATION GUIDE

Aborigines (a-buh-RIH-juh-neez): Australia's native peoples

Aoraki (ow-RAHK-ee): the original Maori name for Aoraki/Mount Cook

biodiversity: a wide range of plants and animals living in a specific place

coral reefs: undersea structures formed from the outer skeletons of marine animals

Dreamtime: in Aboriginal culture, the time when ancient spirit ancestors, such as the Rainbow Serpent, created Earth. Dreamtime is also called Creation Time.

equator: the imaginary line that divides the globe into northern and southern hemispheres

flora: a region's plant life

geology: the study of Earth's soil and rocks. Geologists study layers of soil and rocks to understand Earth's history and how its natural processes work.

Gondwana (gahn-DWAH-nuh): a prehistoric supercontinent, or huge landmass

Kanak (KAH-nahk): one of the original peoples of New Caledonia

Kilauea (KEE-lah-way-ah): a volcano on the Hawaiian island of Hawaii

lava: the hot, melted rock that explodes from or flows out of an active volcano

Maori (MOW-ree): the original people of New Zealand

marsupials: animals, such as a kangaroo, that carry their young in a pouchlike sack

Melanesia (meh-luh-NEE-zhuh): a group of islands in Oceania east of Australia

Micronesia (my-kruh-NEE-zhuh): a group of small islands east of the Philippines

Oceania (oh-shee-AH-nee-uh): the general name given to the many islands of the central and South Pacific Ocean east of Australia

Outback: the remote areas of interior Australia where few people live

Pacific Plate: a tectonic plate—a huge slab of rock on Earth's surface—that lies beneath the Pacific Ocean

Polynesia (pah-luh-NEE-zhuh): a group of islands in the eastern and northern part of Oceania

rain forest: a densely wooded region that normally gets more than 160 inches (406 centimeters) of rain a year

Southern Hemisphere: the half of the globe south of the equator

temperate: a climate that does not have extremes of weather

United Nations Educational, Scientific, and Cultural Organization (UNESCO): a branch of the United Nations, an international organization devoted to cooperation among countries. UNESCO's World Heritage Centre identifies and helps protect and preserve sites that are part of the world's cultural and natural heritage.

volcano: an opening in Earth's surface that releases melted rock, ash, and gas

wilderness: land where few humans live

SOURCE NOTES

9   Bill Bryson, *In a Sunburned Country* (New York: Broadway Books, 2000), 6.

21   Maori proverb, quoted in *Explore Te Ara: The Encyclopedia of New Zealand,*" 2007, http://www.TeAra.govt.nz/TheBush/Landscapes/Mountains/5/en (February 10, 2008).

28   William Ellis, quoted in *Narrative Tour of Volcano,* 2006, http://www.coffeetimes.com/WilliamEllis.html (February 1, 2008).

33   Mark Twain, *Roughing It* (1866, repr., New York: Penguin Books, 2003), 398.

37   UNESCO World Heritage, "Purnululu National Park," 2003, http://whc.unesco.org/en/list/1094 (July 16, 2007).

45   Gustav Weindorfer, quoted in John Man and Chris Schuler, *The Traveler's Atlas* (Hauppage, NY: Barron's Educational Services, 1998), 194.

48   Abel Tasman, quoted in J. J. de H. Labillardière, "The Wilderness Society: Defending Australia's Wild Country," *The Wilderness Society,* 2001, http://www.wilderness.org.au/campaigns/forests/tasmania/ftfquotes/ (February 3, 2008).

59   Louis-Antoine Comte de Bougainville, quoted in Robin Hanbury-Tenison, *The Oxford Book of Exploration* (Oxford: Oxford University Press, 1993), 402.

60   James A. Michener, quoted in George Ridge, "Island Paradise Grapples with Infrastructure" *International Herald Tribune,* October 9, 1995, http://www.iht.com/articles/1995/10/09/bora.php (February 24, 2008).

64   Cheryll Greenwood Kinsley, "Plant of the Month: Amborella Trichopoda," *Washington State University: Whatcom County Extension,* March 2000, http://whatcom.wsu.edu/ag/homehort/plant/amborella.html (February 23, 2008).

67   Eric Dinerstein, quoted in Mark McGinley, ed., "The Encyclopedia of Earth: New Caledonia Rain Forests," *World Wildlife Fund,* March 19, 2007, http://www.eoearth.org/article/New_Caledonia-rain-forests (February 20, 2008).

SELECTED BIBLIOGRAPHY

Barnes-Svarney, Patricia L., and Thomas E. Svarney. *The Oryx Guide to Natural History: The Earth and All Its Inhabitants*. Phoenix: Oryx Press, 1999.

Barrow, John, ed. *Captain Cook's Voyages of Discovery*. New York: Dutton, 1941.

Cleare, John. *Mountains of the World*. San Diego: Thunder Bay Press, 1997.

De Boer, Jelle Zeilinga, and Donald Theodore Sanders. *Volcanoes in Human History: The Far-Reaching Effects of Major Eruptions*. Princeton, NJ: Princeton University Press, 2002.

Flannery, Tim. *The Explorers: Stories of Discovery and Adventure from the Australian Frontier*. New York: Grove Press, 1998.

Gates, Alexander E., and David Ritchie. *Encyclopedia of Earthquakes and Volcanoes*. New York: Checkmark Books, 2007.

Hanbury-Tenison, Robin. *The Oxford Book of Exploration*. Oxford: Oxford University Press, 1993.

Hancock, Paul, and Brian J. Skinner, eds. *The Oxford Companion to the Earth*. Oxford: Oxford University Press, 2000.

Luhr, James F., ed. *Earth*. London: Dorling Kindersley, 2003.

Macintyre, Stuart. *A Concise History of Australia*. Cambridge: Cambridge University Press, 2004.

Man, John, and Chris Schuler. *The Traveler's Atlas*. Hauppage, NY: Barron's Educational Services, 1998.

Moore, Robert J., Jr. *Natural Wonders of the World*. New York: Abbeville Press, 2000.

Peters, Dave. "Hot Times on the Big Island." *Minneapolis Star-Tribune*, June 15, 2008, section G.

FURTHER READING AND WEBSITES

Books

Arnold, Caroline. *Uluru: Australia's Aboriginal Heart.* New York: Clarion Books, 2003. Beautiful photographs show the landscape and animals of Uluru-Kata Tjuta National Park in the middle of the Australian continent.

Bartlett, Anne. *The Aboriginal Peoples of Australia.* Minneapolis: Lerner Publications Company, 2001. Barlett looks at the history and culture of Australia's first peoples and their strong connection to the land.

Bright, Michael. *1001 Natural Wonders You Must See Before You Die.* Hauppauge, NY: Barron's, 2005. This guide will lead you to all the wonderful natural wonders around the world. It includes descriptions of these wonders as well as an explanation of how they were formed.

Burt, Denise. *Kangaroos.* Minneapolis: Lerner Publications Company, 2000. As part of the Nature Watch series, Burt's book looks at the marsupial that has become a symbol of the Australian Outback.

DiPiazza, Francesca. *New Zealand in Pictures.* Minneapolis: Twenty-First Century Books, 2006. This book details the geography, history, culture, and economy of New Zealand.

Kerns, Ann. *Australia in Pictures.* Minneapolis: Twenty-First Century Books, 2004. This book examines Australia's geography, history, culture, and unique natural beauty.

Leppman, Elizabeth J. *Australia and the Pacific.* Philadelphia: Chelsea House, 2006. Part of the World Culture series, this book focuses on Australia and the Pacific region. It gives an overview of the unique landscape and the various cultures that make up this region of the world.

Markle, Sandra. *Tasmanian Devils.* Minneapolis: Lerner Publications Company, 2005. Part of the Animal Scavenger series, this book looks at the life cycle and habits of Tasmania's unique marsupials.

Theunissen, Steve. *The Maori of New Zealand.* Minneapolis: Lerner Publications Company, 2002. Theunissen looks at the history and culture of New Zealand's first people.

Walker, Sally M. *Rays.* Minneapolis: Lerner Publications Company, 2002. This Nature Watch book examines a variety of these strange marine creatures, including the giant manta ray.

Woods, Michael, and Mary B. Woods. *Volcanoes.* Minneapolis: Lerner Publications Company, 2006. Learn about how volcanoes form in Earth and the amount of destruction that an erupting volcano causes.

Websites

Culture.gov.au

http://www.cultureandrecreation.gov.au/
The Australian government's culture and recreation website offers a wide variety of information about history, the environment, Aboriginal culture, the School of the Air, bushwalking, and many other Australian topics.

The Hawaiian Volcano Observatory: Kilauea

http://hvo.wr.usgs.gov/kilauea/
This United States Geological Survey website includes a history of Kilauea, maps, an eruption summary, and other information. The website also includes links to Mauna Loa and about other volcanoes in the world.

Hillman Wonders of the World

http://www.hillmanwonders.com/
This website contains a long list of world wonders from travel expert Howard Hillman. The main list is a mix of ancient, modern, and natural wonders. Each entry describes a wonder and why it is special.

Unique Australian Animals

http://australian-animals.net/
This site provides photos and information about Australia's native animals. Learn about echidnas, thorny devils, frilled lizards, kangaroos, koalas, and many more.

Visual Geography Series

http://www.vgsbooks.com/
This extension of Lerner Publishing Group's Visual Geography Series® (VGS) is a one-stop resource for links to additional country specific information, up-to-date statistics, photographs and maps that can be downloaded, and much more.

World Heritage List

http://whc.unesco.org/en/list/
Organized by countries, UNESCO's World Heritage List includes natural and historic sites. Each site's page includes a map, a description of the site, a photo gallery, and a list of dangers threatening the site.

INDEX

ABOUT THE AUTHORS

Michael Woods is a science journalist in Washington, D.C., who has won many national writing awards. Mary B. Woods is a librarian in the Fairfax County Public School System in Virginia. Their previous books include the eight-volume Ancient Technology series and the fifteen-volume Disasters Up Close series. The Woodses have four children. When not writing, reading, or enjoying their grandchildren, they travel to gather material for future books.

PHOTO ACKNOWLEDGMENTS

The images in this book are used with the permission of: © Mitsuaki Iwago/Minden Pictures/Getty Images, pp. 4, 47 (bottom); © William L. Allen/National Geographic/Getty Images, p. 5; © Neil Emmerson/Robert Harding/drr.net, p. 6; © Nigel Dickinson/drr.net, p. 8; © Chris McGrath/Getty Images, p. 10; © Palani Mohan/Getty Images, p. 11 (main); © Bill Bachmann/Danita Delimont Agency/drr.net, p. 11 (inset); © iStockphoto.com/MarzenaWasilewska, p. 12; © Konrad Wothe/Minden Pictures/Getty Images, pp. 13, 15 (bottom right); © Ian Waldie/Getty Images, p. 14; © S. K. Patrick/Visuals Unlimited, Inc., p. 15 (top left); © Royalty-Free/CORBIS, p. 15 (top right); © iStockphoto.com/Pauline Mills, p. 15 (bottom left); © Belinda Wright/National Geographic/Getty Images, p. 16; © iStockphoto.com/Steve Lovegrove, p. 17; © iStockphoto.com/Fredrik Larsson, p. 18; © iStockphoto.com/HarryKolenbrander, pp. 20, 25 (inset); © Julia Thorne/Robert Harding/drr.net, p. 21; © JTB Photo/drr.net, pp. 24, 68; © James W. Kay/drr.net, p. 25 (main); © Greg Vaughn/drr.net, p. 26; © Chris Johns/National Geographic/Getty Images, p. 29; © Science VU/USGS/Visuals Unlimited, Inc., p. 31; © dave jepson 1/Alamy, p. 32; © Photo Resource Hawaii/Danita Delimont Agency/drr.net, p. 33; © imagebroker/Alamy, p. 34; © Nordicphotos/Alamy, p. 36; ©Trevor Phillips, p. 38; © Jean-Paul Ferrero/AUSCAPE/The Image Works, pp. 40, 45, 69; © Richard Ashworth/Robert Harding/drr.net, p. 41; © James Osmond/Photographer's Choice RR/Getty Images, p. 42; © iStockphoto.com/Keiichi Hiki, pp. 44, 46; © Bill Bachman/Alamy, p. 47 (top); © Christian Kober/Robert Harding/drr.net, p. 49; © Jochen Schlenker/Robert Harding World Imagery/Getty Images, p. 51; © Wolfgang Kaehler/Gallo Images/Getty Images, p. 52; © Art Wolfe/The Image Bank/Getty Images, p. 55 (main); © Spaceimaging.com/Getty Images, p. 55 (inset); © Art Wolfe/Danita Delimont Agency/drr.net, p. 56; © Raphael Van Butsele/Photographer's Choice/Getty Images, p. 57 (top left); © Hemis.fr/SuperStock, p. 57 (top right); © Michele Westmorland/drr.net, p. 57 (bottom); © age fotostock/SuperStock, p. 59; © Paul Timpa/Dreamstime.com, p. 60; © Jean-Marc Truchet/Riser/Getty Images, p. 61; © Altrendo/Getty Images, pp. 62, 64; © Martin/Andia.fr/drr.net, p. 65; © BCS/Alamy, p. 66; © David Northcott/Danita Delimont.com/drr.net, p. 67 (main); © Bourget/Andia.fr/drr.net, p. 67 (inset); © Robert W. Madden /National Geographic/Getty Images, p. 72 (top left); © Sylvester Adams/Digital Vision/Getty Images, p. (top center); © AA World Travel Library /Alamy, p. 72 (top right); © Jean-Bernard Carillet /Lonely Planet Images /Getty Images, p. 72 (bottom left); © Waltraud/snapvillage, p. 72 (bottom center); © Craig Lovell/Stock Connection/drr.net, p. 72 (bottom right); © iStockphoto.com/czardases, p. 72 (center right). Illustrations by © Laura Westlund/Independent Picture Service.

Front cover: © Jean-Bernard Carillet /Lonely Planet Images/Getty Images (top left); © Waltraud/snapvillage (top center); © Robert W. Madden /National Geographic/Getty Images (top right); © iStockphoto.com/czardases (center); © AA World Travel Library / Alamy (bottom left); © Sylvester Adams/Digital Vision/Getty Images (bottom center); © Craig Lovell/Stock Connection/drr.net (bottom right).